Living With A Momma's Boy

Learn how to position yourself to be his #1 priority

Sheri A. Brooks
and
Glenn P. Brooks, Jr.
Author of "How To Raise A Man...Not A Momma's Boy!"

Living With A Momma's Boy

Learn how to position yourself to be his #1 priority

Sheri A. Brooks
and
Glenn P. Brooks, Jr.

Copyright © 2013

ISBN-13: 978-1482597035
ISBN-10: 1482597039
Printed in the United States of America

For more information visit us online at
www.GlennPBrooksJr.com
www.constantrelationshipcoaching.com

Living With A Momma's Boy

DEDICATION

This book is dedicated to every woman who has ever or is currently dating, courting or is married to a man who was left to raise himself.

In order to have the best relationship possible you need to understand the man in your life. Our goal is to challenge your perception of what a Momma's Boy is and also help you better understand this mindset so that you can have a healthy and functional relationship.

Contents

Living With A Momma's Boy

INTRODUCTION

A few words from Glenn P. Brooks, Jr.,

Shortly after the release of my book "How To Raise A Man … Not A Momma's Boy!" the following question was presented to me. I can't remember exactly where I first heard it, but women kept asking and it became a re-occurring question "How do I live with a Momma's Boy?" As it turns out many women that I come across that have read my book or been in a seminar/workshop that I have taught are coming to the same conclusion. That is that "many of the men that they live with" (be it their boyfriend, husband, or brother) "display the characteristics of what I define as a momma's boy." My definition of a Momma's Boy is a man who thinks, acts, and sometimes behaves emotionally like a woman.

As I pondered that question, I realized that like myself a recovering Momma's Boy there are many men who have been raised in an environment without the presence of strong healthy men. Men who were intentionally, loving, and consistently available to nurture, lead, and protect their boys.

So I sat down and asked my wife of 14 years how did you do it? How did you live with a Momma's Boy? She laughed and gently reminded me that she not only lived with one but two Momma's Boys. The second one was my son from a previous marriage who also was raised in an environment without a healthy father for the first twelve years of his life. See my first wife and I separated before my son turned two years old. I was the weekend dad. You know every other weekend and two weeks in the summer consistently. Although I paid my child support it did not replace the absence of my presence. The consequence of my being missing-in-action did not show up until he was a preteen and it was at that time that he came to live with my wife and I full-time.

I quickly learned firsthand the damage caused when men are missing-in-action in the lives of boys. Even though I grew up without my dad and later learned how that affected my life, it was very hard to see that I had done the same things to my own son. A father's role is to lead, protect, provide, encourage, discipline, nurture, and instruct and because my father was missing-in-action and I didn't get these things I in turn did the same thing when I rolled out on my son.

So going back to the question that I asked my wife: "how did you do it, how did you live with a Momma's Boys and not lose your mind?" My wife was a divorced single mother who raised a daughter for 12 years before we got married, so when we got together we became a blended family. She has been an integral part of my/our son's life for the past 16 years and I have been a full time father to her/our daughter. She possesses the experience as a single parent and a "step-parent" which gives her a great perspective on men and boys. Throughout this book she is going to share with you the wisdom she gained over the years that helped her to live with her Momma's Boys. She will share exactly how she did it and my hope is that somehow through our transparency you will gain some insight on how to live with the Momma's Boys in your life.

A few words from Sheri A. Brooks

First off I want to thank my husband and best-friend, Glenn P. Brooks Jr., for embracing the voice that I have developed over the years and for being willing to change for the better. With that being said I want you all to know that it has taken me years to come to many of the conclusions I share in this book. There were many days I wanted to pull my hair out and even cried myself to sleep. As I reflected over my past relationships I can admit that the majority of the boys/men who I was involved with all had some Momma's Boy traits, whether they were raised in a single parent home or had two parents. When I met Glenn he was a "man on a mission". He was successful in his field and he was a great leader.   His Momma's Boy traits were not apparent and it was not until a few years into our marriage that I began to see them.. At the same time I was co-parenting our son who was also displaying some of these traits at a young age.   The challenges of dealing with not one but two Momma's Boys intensified when our son came to live with us full-time. Over the years I had built a relationship with him from a distance, but I had never raised a boy, and especially not a boy who had been raised as a Momma's Boy. So ladies, I understand the pain of not only living with a grown man who was raised to be a Momma's Boy, but I also have had a "birds-eye" view of what it looks like in its formative stage. Before we go on, one thing you will notice is that I refer to our son as just that "our son", even though we are a blended family we don't subscribe to the traditional "step-parent" roles. I have been actively involved in our son's life since he was four years old and have had an excellent co-parenting relationship with his mother and her husband. Unfortunately when he came to live with us it became apparent to us that he had missed out on some of the fundamentals of manhood training.

Today it amazes me to watch him grow and utilize the tools he has learned over the years to be assertive and responsible today. My husband has also put in the work to rid himself of most of his Momma's Boy tendencies and I am very proud of the man he is today and continues to grow into daily. Today I am grateful for all the misunderstandings and disagreements we have experienced over the years. I couldn't see it then but every challenge was developing character and perseverance in me and was helping to shape the Momma's Boys in my life into the men they are today. I welcome you to join me as I share some of the insights I gained over the years dealing with my Momma's Boys and how I was able to live with them and not lose my mind!

This book was birthed out of our personal relationship and parenting experiences, in addition to almost 20 years of working with youth and helping other parents, whether single parents, traditional families or blended families work through the challenges of marriage and raising their children. Glenn and I will both share throughout the book. My highlights and points will be labeled as From A Woman's Perspective and *How To Live With A Momma's Boy* and Glenn's highlights and points will be labeled From A Man's Perspective and *Tips For Dealing With A Momma's Boy.*

Living With A Momma's Boy

1

MOMMA'S BOY MYTHS

When you hear the term Momma's Boy there may be a myriad of thoughts that go through your mind. I want to first dispel a few myths about what a Momma's Boy is not before we go any further. Glenn describes a Momma's Boy as a male who emotionally thinks, responds, and in some cases behaves like a female. The key word to remember here is emotionally. Before we go any further let's clear some of the myths about a Momma's Boy.

Myth #1: Nurturing your son will make him a wimp.

Nurturing your son does not create a Momma's Boy. All children need to be nurtured by their parents. By definition nurturing is simply caring and encouraging the growth and development of your child. What nurturing is NOT is controlling your child. Parents who control their children use their position to direct or manage their behavior. When a mother is controlling, she will manage every aspect of her son's life, thus making him dependent on her for every simple task. At ten your son should be able to make his bed and clean his bedroom, but the controlling mother won't let him because he doesn't do it the way she would. This teaches him that he can't do anything right and eventually he will stop trying and when asked to do things he will put little effort if any into to accomplishing the task.

Nurturing mothers are loving and caring and teach their sons that it is okay to feel, be in touch with your emotions, and how to put others first. The challenge comes in when this is out of balance. One extreme is the controlling mother and the other is the mother who dotes on her son (*lavishes excessive attention, fondness, or affection*). This excessive affection can create a boy who grows up expecting to be the center of attention in every relationship.

Myth # 2: Boys raised by single mothers are Momma's Boys.

A boy being raised by a single mother is not a guarantee that he will become a Momma's Boy. I know several men who were raised in two parent households who are Momma's Boys. Even though their fathers were in the home he was either preoccupied or their mothers were controlling. Momma's Boys are often the by-product of not having a strong and healthy father or father figure. This lack of a strong male presence often times causes a void in his development. When he should be allowed to explore and figure things out, he is often times stifled by his mother, out of her fear of him getting hurt or her inability to teach him "man things". A single mother can provide her son with a strong and healthy male presence by encouraging his involvement in organized sports, connecting him with a male mentor, or allowing him to spend constant and consistent time with his father, other male family members, or friends who are positive healthy male role models.

Boys need men to show them how to be a man. Just like the little duck in the children's book "Are you my mother" by P. D. Eastman, boys will search for someone to identify with and emulate that behavior. If he is around passive, lazy, non-caring males he will emulate this behavior and associate that as how a man is "supposed to be". In a perfect world boys would be raised by Ward Cleaver or Cliff Huxtable. In our world there are some real dads who are actively involved in their children's lives, and plenty of male coaches, teachers, and mentors who are willing to encourage, discipline, instruct and love them.

Mother's here's a tip – you CAN NOT raise your son to be a man! Think about it, just like you can't teach him how to aim and urinate standing up – there are just some things that ONLY a man can teach your son.

Myth # 3: Momma's Boys grow up to be homosexual men.

This is simply not true. Although some boys raised in a predominantly female environment will display effeminate qualities ... that is not an assurance that he will be gay. Being a Momma's Boy has nothing to do with his sexuality. It has everything to do with the environment that he is shaped in. An environment void of men will emotionally shape the way your son thinks and in many cases behaves. He'll many times lack the "dare" to step out and take on new challenges. His tendency will be to wait and see what happens. He will develop a passive approach as a result of being raised in an environment lacking a consistent positive male influence.

Boys tend to be naturally aggressive and want to run over, jump on, and climb things. It doesn't matter what it is, the bigger the better, they just want to conquer. If he is around men this type of behavior is encouraged over and over again, but in the presence of women he is often made to "sit down and behave". Glenn shares in his book "How To Raise A Man...Not A Momma's Boy!" that when he was growing up most people thought he was rambunctious and talkative. He recalls his mother telling him to sit down and shut up so often that he actually thought his first name was "sit down" and his last name was "shut up". Looking back at this he can now laugh, but this type of control stunted his growth in some key areas of his life.

When a boy is allowed to express himself through very active play, he learns something about himself; he learns limits, strength, assertiveness and confidence. These are all qualities that most women love and want in their man. When you're in relationship with a man who doesn't possess some of these qualities, often time it's as a result of him growing up in an environment where he was not allowed to explore and develop. You see there is this chemical called testosterone that courses through his veins, and when it's bottled up as a young boy and not allowed out, sometimes it produces a passive but aggressive man. Testosterone is not a crime. It shouldn't be made to be punishable by an evil look or controlling words.

Myth # 4: Momma's Boys will ALWAYS be "Mommy's little boy"

Our culture typically refers to the guys who still live at home well into their twenties and thirties as Momma's Boys. These are the men who let their mothers wash their clothes and cook their meals, while they live at home with little if any responsibility. That is one form of a Momma's Boy. However, in my travels this is the exception more so than the rule.

Most of the Momma's Boys I have encountered had mother's who pushed them out of the nest. Now some of them were not adequately prepared for adulthood, but in most cases they figured it out. In the few cases I have seen when the man remained at home as grown Momma's Boy it was because the mother had an emotional void that she was filling that prevented her from releasing her son to the world. It is a normal transition for children to leave home at a certain point in their development so that they can mature and become productive adults.

Men who remain home into adulthood and have no desire to venture off on their own have been stifled in their growth in some areas, which makes it hard for them to find their own identity outside of "mommy dearest". On the other hand boys who are raised to become men by their mothers typically develop into self sufficient men who make loving and caring husbands. The years of being cared for by their mothers may have given them an appreciation and respect for women which they will take into their future relationships.

Living With A Momma's Boy

2

WHAT IS A MAN?

If you ask this question to 100 people you will inevitably get varying answers. Magazines depict him as a perfectly chiseled specimen of a man to be worshipped. Movies often portray him as being an insensitive jerk, who doesn't know what to say out of his mouth. He is useless without a woman to take care of him, and he is clueless that this type of behavior is unacceptable. He is often motivated by sex, alcohol, and money. Television shows give even more varying images, from the openly gay father to the single father who has no self-worth and free loads off his family and friends to support himself and his children. When we were growing up the images of a man were primarily fathers and husbands who provided for and spent time with their families. These images helped to shape our perspectives along with our personal experiences. In order to answer this question we interviewed men and women to get their perspective on "What is a man?"

From a woman's perspective:

Over the past year I have interviewed a variety of women from different walks of life and have compiled a list of the top things that both single and married women say make up a man.

- ❖ A man is a protector; he is selfless and puts the concerns of his loved ones above his own. He will give his life for his family.

- ❖ A man is a provider; he will do whatever he needs to do in order to ensure his loved ones are cared for.

- ❖ A man is a fixer; when problems arise he will figure out how to fix it.

❖ A man takes responsibility for his actions; when he screws up he admits it, changes and moves on.

❖ A man loves intentionally; when he commits he is committed, he will love the ground you walk on.

❖ A man needs affirmation and encouragement. No matter how strong he may seem to be he needs to know he is doing a good job.

❖ A man is in touch with his emotions and can express them. He is not afraid to cry or say when he is hurt.

❖ A man is a leader; he will lead his family in the direction of his vision for the family.

❖ A man is gentle; he will not harm those he loves. He will speak truth in love and control his anger.

From a man's perspective:

As a man I find it interesting to hear the perspective of women as they identify the things they believe make up a man, and I totally agree.

But in addition to that I would add the following qualities:

❖ A man encourages - he knows what to say or do when necessary to build the self esteem of his family and those he loves.

❖ He instructs - he doesn't bark out orders but educates. He takes time to slow down and communicate what he needs.

❖ A man serves - he practices putting others first. He is constantly looking to see how he can add value to those he is connected to.

❖ And although a man learns to become this – A true man nurtures. A real man will express how much he cares by his actions and not simply by his words.

Now I know some of you may be beginning to figure out that your man or the men in your life do not possess some or most of these qualities. You may be coming to the realization that because they were not raised by a man there are some fundamental "man things" that are missing. Even without the presence of a physical father there is hope for them to become the men they were ultimately designed to be. Becoming a man is more than simply turning eighteen, it is about maturing and maturity is not something that is defined by age. In my opinion maturity is a process of development that occurs as a result of the responsibilities and trials of life. A person who has never had to be responsible or make any decisions will still think as a child and be dependent on others.

"When I was a child, I talked like a child. I thought like a child, I reasoned like a

child. When I became a man, I put the ways of childhood behind me." 1 *Corinthians 31:11*

In the next few chapters I will describe a few types of Momma's Boys so that you can identify who you are dealing with and give you some tips on how to live with him without losing your mind. We hope to show you it is possible to love and embrace who he is and create an environment that he can grow into the man he was designed to be.

Living With A Momma's Boy

3

HOW TO IDENTIFY A MOMMA'S BOY

Now that we have dispelled some myths and given you some general views on what a man is, you may be wondering what do I do next.

We will discuss four types of Momma's Boys. As an adult the Momma's Boy can be hard to identify. Why because he has learned to become a chameleon, he has become good at changing and adapting to his environment in order to fit in. It is easier to recognize the Momma's Boy as a child, because his qualities will be more obvious. In many cases he is very selfish and has an entitlement mindset. He can also be somewhat sheepish, meaning he is usually a follower and not the leader of the pack. As an adult the Momma's Boy may often appear to be confident, caring, and selfless initially. This is primarily because these have become tools that he has developed in order to mask his inadequacies. Please understand that he has practiced over his lifetime covering up these inadequacies, so don't beat yourself up if you don't catch these things in the beginning of your relationship. He has become good at this over time, but it's not malicious and he doesn't mean to deceive you. It has become a defense mechanism. Over time as they begin to deal with the stresses of life and work you may begin to see signs of his Momma's Boy tendencies.

The four types of Momma's Boys we will be discussing are *Mr. People Pleaser, Mr. Time Bomb, Mr. Narcissist,* and *Mr. Sensitive*.

The people pleaser is the man who can't seem to tell you how he really feels or what he thinks because he is more concerned with pleasing you than telling you the truth. The time bomb is the passive aggressive man. He holds things in and never shares how he really feels. In other words he will hold things in until the pressure builds up and then he will explode leaving a mess for everyone else to clean up. Then we have the narcissist, he is the "ME" guy. It is all about him... all the time. He is the guy you can be in a conversation with and it always seems to turn into a conversation about him. And lastly we have the sensitive man. He has gotten so in touch with his feminine side that he allows his emotions to rule him.

As we move forward through this book we want you to recognize and understand the common thread through all Momma's

Boys. They tend to be men who are immature and underdeveloped in certain areas. At some point in time in their development as boys they stopped growing emotionally due to neglect or abuse. This resulted in their staying in a perpetual state of boyhood, even though he has aged chronologically in many ways he still processes like a little boy. Some clear signs of this are a man who is fearful, passive, angry, and bitter.

At first glance you may not be able to readily identify these qualities with the Momma's Boy in your life, but I invite you to sit back and take this ride with us as we expose some truths behind Momma's Boys and how you can truly have a healthy and functional relationship with these men if you are willing to put in a little work.

4

MR. PEOPLE PLEASER

Momma's Boys can be loyal to a fault. They can be so consumed in pleasing people that they lose sight of their own personal needs and the needs of their family. Because many Momma's Boys were raised without solid relationships with their fathers or a strong father figure in their lives they crave and need the affirmation of men or people who they consider to be authority figures in their life. This craving causes him to say "yes" in situations when he should say "no". This comes out of his need to be liked and his fear of rejection.

Mr. People Pleaser makes a great friend because of his loyalties and his desire to make those that he is in relationship with happy. See a people pleaser lacks the ability to be honest with himself. In other words, he tells himself what he wants to hear and accepts things as he wants them to be as opposed to how they really are. A people pleaser will be in the midst of dealing with a family issue and get a call from a friend and will not only take it but divert his focus to their issue rather than putting his family first. He will take valuable time away from his family in order to meet the needs of a friend because he doesn't want his friend to feel that he is not there for them. His need to be accepted and be a part of something can sometime outweigh his need to be a part of his family. In this case major boundaries are crossed because people pleasers have no concept of boundaries. Boundaries are like fences. They are put up to protect and mark off specific areas to keep them separate. In their book "Boundaries" Henry Cloud and John Townsend define a boundary as a property line, it denotes the beginning and the end of something.

The people pleaser will be your biggest cheerleader because he is legitimately excited to see you win. He will cheer you on in his attempt to make sure you know that he is in your corner which makes him feel like a valuable part of your life. This can be displayed on the job and is sometimes labeled as the "brown noser". His need to be accepted will make him the spokesman for others good deeds. Unfortunately this is all motivated by his own unquenched need for affirmation and approval which will often cause him to forsake his own personal goals or beliefs in order to be accepted. He will oftentimes lack the motivation to do things independently due to his need for constant approval. He can be so driven by his need to please that he will overlook being taken advantage of or even mistreated. This Momma's Boy can sometimes become a doormat and take abuse either verbally, physically, or emotionally or all three – always excusing the abuser because of his low self worth outside of the approval he believes he needs from them. This is actually a false sense of belonging because his worth is based solely off of his meeting the expectations of others and not based on his own personal acceptance of who he is.

How to live with Mr. People Pleaser:

The first step to living with a people pleaser is recognizing that the need for approval and affirmation is a real need, especially for men. Having been a single parent for years it was hard for me to give affirmation to a man who I believed should come in and do what "men do". This was where I made my first mistake, I had subscribed to a fairytale that ALL men are supposed to work all day, bring home the big check, fix things around the house, romance their wives, listen to how my day went and do this all with a smile. As much as I believed my husband was my knight in shining honor and I had these high expectations of him. I failed to ask him what his expectations were of being a husband or of me as a wife. Needless to say that it came as total shock to me when he did not volunteer to fix the leaky sink or take out the trash. This resulting in my fussing about the things I needed him to do and constantly telling him what I didn't like. This led to some very frustrating years in the beginning of our marriage.

The funny thing is that as I look back on how he cared for his own things before we got married, I would have seen that at work he was very different than he was at home. By this I mean he was polished at work, he got things done but this was all attributed to the fact that he got praise for doing a great job in the way of bonuses and recognition. At home he was much more lackadaisical about his business, he paid bills late and his home was not very tidy. Now his personal appearance was immaculate but that was also because he got something out of keeping up a good outer appearance.

When I finally realized that his need for approval and affirmation was real I had to make a few changes to my approach. Recognizing that he was not trying to manipulate me into giving him an "attaboy" just for the heck of it, he really needed to hear when he was doing a good job. This required me to stop associating what he did with who he was. As women we can have a tendency to tell a man that he is no good because he is lacking or missing something in one area. I learned that a man's ego is very fragile, as strong as they may seem to be on the outside they really do have feelings. When you tear a man down with your words it is very hard to take those words back and they cause scars that will last for years.

It is a pretty good assumption that his need for affirmation and approval may be increased because he didn't receive any during his upbringing which has contributed to his becoming a Momma's Boy. If he was raised by a controlling mother the last thing he needs is to be tongue lashed every time he comes home. So choose your words carefully. Speak truth in love, and deal with issues but DO NOT tear him down with your words. His actions are just that, actions. They are not who he is no more than you are what you do.

Next I had to recognize that the people pleaser in him was the result of him having some unfulfilled needs as a child and admit that I could not give him what he missed nor could I fix him. It was not my responsibility to make up for this deficit but I could provide him with affirmation when it was appropriate without further enabling him in his dysfunction. Now let me say this - it is almost impossible for you to do this if you are a people pleaser yourself. If you are honest with yourself there is a little people pleaser in all of us, but if you don't get yours under control you both are in a world of trouble. Your people pleasing tendencies may look very different than his. Women tend to please those they are closest to. In the movie "Coming to America" the main character is presented with a potential bride who is the epitome of a people pleaser. Whenever he asked her what she wanted, her response was always "Whatever you like!" This is an extreme case but she clearly did not know what her own wants or needs were and she was only concerned with pleasing him. People pleasers get something out of it when they do for others. It is more about how it makes them feel needed than really doing for the other person.

People pleasing men often tend to please their loved ones in an effort to keep the peace. So he may avoid confronting you on something that he disagrees with or has an issue with because he doesn't like conflict. He is more consumed with what you think than what is really true. He will go along to get along. He may not be overly agreeable but you will sense that at times he is just going along not to hear your mouth. This is a clear indication that he is in *pleaser mode*. In order to help your man come out of this you have to create an environment that he feels safe to share what he really thinks. This goes back to your choosing your words again. If you have to hold your tongue every now and then to get him to tell you the truth isn't it worth it? When a man feels that he is respected and his opinion matters he will be more apt to share.

In my case I was a rescuer and people pleaser myself so I had to address my own need to please and rescue before I could attempt to address this issue in the relationship. Once I was able to admit to myself that I got something out of doing things for people, because it made me feel needed and important. I was able to begin my process and the first step was learning to say "no". The hardest part in learning to say no was learning what I liked. I had been saying "yes" to please others for so long I had to discover what I liked and disliked. This gave me a sense of freedom. I was free to say "no" to the things I didn't want to do and the freedom to ask for what I wanted. Now there is a balance in all of this, you have to be careful not to go from one extreme to the other. I still do things for those I love and will even choose to go along with something they want to do but it is no longer motivated out of my need to feel needed, but out of my willingness to compromise.

Once I learned how not to be a people pleaser myself I was then able to speak truth to my mate in love. See not telling your people pleaser how you really feel when they are off saving the world, running to the rescue of their friends and family, or appeasing you by going along with everything you say can lead to bitterness and resentment. This can be difficult at first because people pleasers will often times try to avoid conflict and not want to deal with the real issues. Remember they are people pleasers and you are one of the main people they want to please, so they will try to please you in order to keep the peace.

The key to helping your man break from the people pleaser is to affirm him and remind him of who he is outside of the things he does. Create a safe environment for him to feel free to share how he really feels about anything, and when you disagree do it respectfully. Don't turn a disagreement into an attack on his character as a man. Tell him how you really feel in love and remind him of how great a father or husband he is every chance you get and watch him rise to the occasion.

Tips for dealing with Mr. People Pleaser:

My wife is 100% correct. You must constantly deal with Mr. People Pleaser in truth because I have a tendency to see life as I want it to be and not as it is. I have "blind spots" just like a driver needs his side mirrors to know what's in the lane beside him; your man needs your honest perspective. You have to find a way to speak truth to him in love. For example: he is putting way too much time in at work, constantly at the beck and call of any and everything that goes wrong. He's putting his work before you and the family. Now rather than just go along "if it really bothers you" you have to find a way to let him know how it truly makes you feel. NOTE: Don't try this in the heat of an argument … it will not go well. Find a noncrisis moment to explain to him that when he does "_____" it makes you feel like "____" (fill in the blanks and be specific)! He needs to know how his people pleasing behavior is damaging the relationship. If he's anything like me he will respond to the "pain" that he sees he is causing you. If you're consistent in pointing this out in "love" and he recognizes it as "love" more often than not he will change, because if he really cares and he really loves you he will not willingly hurt you.

Living With A Momma's Boy

5

MR. NARCISSIST

Mr. Narcissist has the potential to be a great leader. The narcissist is self-centered and has an entitlement mentality. He actually believes that his sh** doesn't stink. He is self-absorbed and finds it hard to believe when others don't understand why he should not get his way. He only wants to do what he wants to do. If you want to go see a play and he wants to watch the game, he will pout or convince you to do what he wants. After all he wants to spend time with you, just as long as you do what he wants. He is often not good with managing the household funds; he tends to be the spender. He typically only spends on himself or on the things he deems important. His entitlement mentality leads him to believe that everyone owes him something. He thinks he should be praised for simply showing up, that alone should be worth something. He rarely thinks about doing things for others unless there is a direct benefit for him. He doesn't believe he should have to sacrifice or that he should have to suffer any consequences for his actions. It is difficult for him to be caring for others, but in his defense he is capable of love. Many times he has difficulty showing love in his actions. Whatever he wants will take precedence over his wife and children and when confronted on his lack of care he will rationalize it away. He believes he deserves to be cared for and he has earned the right to do what he wants, but is unable to be empathetic and put himself in the shoes of others.

To put it plainly, Mr. Narcissist is selfish. He may have grown up in an environment where he was spoiled and always got what he wanted. His mother may have treated him like her little man. He could have been an only child or have other siblings but because of his parents desire to make up for what they lacked as children they created an environment that fostered an entitlement mindset. He may have been raised in a home with a controlling mother who did not allow him to care for himself. This was done in an effort by the mother to maintain control over the household. She may have never allowed him to clean or wash his clothes because she didn't believe he could do it right, so she would do it herself. Whatever the situation he learned that others would do things for him and he has grown up to expect that from everyone including you.

Mr. Narcissist can range from being a total slob who expects others to pick up behind him to being a metro sexual male who primps and cares more about his own appearance than many women care about their appearance. This sometimes makes recognizing him difficult, but rest assured in time you will clearly begin to see that his priority is all about him. There is hope - remember he wants what he wants, so when he has chosen to be with you – that means he wants you. He will do whatever it takes to keep you, sometimes he needs a little reminder to get his priorities in order but there is hope.

How to live with Mr. Narcissist:

Mr. Narcissist is probably the most difficult Momma's Boy to live with. See he has the ability to convince you that you want to go along with him on this ride only for you to look up years later and realize you are on a path you never intended to be on. In most cases you didn't realize just how selfish and self-centered he was when you first met. He was considerate and showed care for your wants and needs, but somehow over time things changed. It may start slowly with small things but overtime you may begin to realize that in his eyes the world revolves around him and his wants. He may show this in his actions subtly by doing things like, stopping to get him something to eat on the way home and forgetting to call and see if you want something. Or he could be more obvious by going out and buying himself all the toys that men like, such as a motorcycle, motorboat, or whatever his thing is, but he doesn't put the same effort into buying gifts for you or anyone else. In most cases it is the little things that over time add up and one day you look up and realize that he hasn't' done anything for you lately. In my Janet Jackson voice "What have you done for me lately?"

The key to living with the narcissist is to clearly and continually communicate what your needs are. He needs to be reminded gently what he needs to do in order to keep the home fires burning. I am not encouraging you to nag or fuss, but I am encouraging you to communicate. This type of man can have a one track mind, and for most of his life that one track was all about him, so you have to help him to include you. A method that I learned early was to show him how I wanted to be treated rather than simply telling him. For instance if my birthday was important to me and I desired for him to make that day special, I would sit down and tell him what

I wanted and then I would do it for myself. Example, if I needed to have a "me" day and felt it would be a great way to celebrate my birthday, I would tell him how much I needed a "me" day and describe what it would look like. I would then schedule myself a massage, manicure, and pedicure. Then I would let him know that we would be going out to dinner that night to celebrate my birthday at my favorite restaurant. Now you may be thinking "well if I have to do it myself what do I need him for?" This is where you have to be patient, after a while he will begin to learn what you desire and he will start to do these things on his own.

I also have been able to use the lines of communication to help him to learn to include me in on any decisions he is making before he makes them. Even though he is the man of the house, we discuss all major purchases in advance. This way there are no surprises, such as a new motorcycle sitting in the driveway when I got home after a day at work. This creates a level of accountability that keeps him from falling back into his old habits of being selfish. I also help him to consider how a purchase affects the entire household and determine whether it is a want or a need. I have to be fair and not shoot down everything he wants while giving a vote of approval for the things I want. We both have to agree on the purchase and honestly decide if it is a valid purchase. We also try to share in all the household tasks so that neither of us gets bogged down with more responsibility than the other. If I cook, he will clean the kitchen or if he puts his clothes in the hamper, I will wash them.

You both have to attempt to make the needs of the other a priority and this only happens when you communicate those needs. If you are in a relationship with a narcissist who truly cares for you he will be willing to give you what you need if he sees that it will benefit him as well. I am sure you have heard the saying that a "happy wife makes a happy life", well this is true and if your man doesn't understand this then there are a few ways you can quickly help him to understand this. There will be times you have to speak his language and use what he needs and desires most in the relationship in order to get what you need and want. Simply put, use your womanly gifts to get what you need by providing him with *"positive reinforcement"*. If he has had a habit of spending money without consulting you – the one time he does consult you be sure to reward him with a very special night.

This seems to motivate most men to think of the needs of their wives. If you need him to fix the bookshelf in your office rather than sit watching the game, parade in the room during halftime in one of his football jerseys and invite him to a game of touch football, and give him a half time show he will never forget. In most cases it will change the frequency of his one track mind to your frequency.

I don't subscribe to withholding the goodies as punishment for his not giving you what you need. There are cases when the behavior of your spouse is harmful to you or he has violated the trust in the relationship when it may be advisable to withhold sexual relations, but this is not the type of behavior we are talking about. In order to get his attention and encourage him, positive reinforcement is often enough to motivate him to make at least a temporary change. And let's be honest we just want him to get on our page long enough for us to get what we want. In time he will understand our needs and we won't have to use such methods, but let's be honest, we enjoy the benefits as well. As stated before a happy wife is the making of a very happy life.

Tips for dealing with Mr. Narcissist:

When my wife and I first met she didn't like me very much, she said I was arrogant and self-centered. She was right. The problem was you couldn't tell me anything. First thing you need to understand about Mr. Narcissist is that for better or for worse he's a very prideful man. He's probably very influential in the circles that he operates in and is very use to having his "EGO" stroked. He typically has a very commanding presence or personality, often that's what caught your attention. The challenge with that is he can appear to be a "Jerk". Often insensitive to other people's individual or personal needs, the world is all about him. Living with this kind of Momma's Boy can be very difficult.

You and your family's needs often get put on the back burner to make room for the project that he's working on that takes up much of his attention. In order to deal with me you MUST and I mean MUST have a life that doesn't revolve around me. Believe it or not the more you "pay close attention to me" the more I'll take you for granted. However as soon as you get a life, I'll all of sudden begin to notice you. Once you have my attention be sure to take advantage of the moment to express to me that you need from me. For example you may have always wanted to go back to school but you have put it off in order to support him and his desires and dreams. I'm encouraging you that if you are able to do it then do it. Go back to school. Get your degree. Do whatever it is that you see in your mind that you need to do that is healthy for you to grow as an individual. When I see that you are no longer sitting around waiting on me and you are taking charge of your life I will sit up and take notice. Over time you're pursuing your dreams will cause me to notice you. In other words since you are positioning yourself as an individual and are no longer totally dependent on me, it will cause me to connect to who you are and what you are doing. If you think about it most successful people are drawn to other successful people. You must remember the narcissist believes his own hype and will be drawn to the new level of confidence you will exude when you are fulfilling one of your passions. It'll take time, but in the end, if I really love you, I'll pay attention, listen, take heed, and switch up in order to give you what you need in the relationship.

6

MR. TIME BOMB

This is the passive aggressive man. The passive side of him will sit there and hear you ask him to take the trash out but will never acknowledge your request because silently his aggressiveness says I refuse to move when she wants me to. He doesn't like to argue so he will avoid conflict at all cost. He will avoid you by coming home late rather than sitting down and talking about an issue. If he is in a relationship with a woman who is controlling, he will act as if everything is ok even though it bothers him for her to yell at him or even dictate to him what he should be doing.

Overtime his time bomb explodes and he will lash out. He may emotionally disconnect from the relationship. He may still physically be there, but he is no longer emotionally connected to the relationship. He may choose to stay because of the children or he may want to keep up the appearance that all is well. At this point he is simply going through the motions. He may lash out by seeking the company of another woman and having an affair as a way to avoid dealing with the real issues as home. If he has anger issue he may lash out by either verbally, emotionally or physically abusing your or the children. No matter how he chooses to lash out if not dealt with this can become a toxic environment.

How to live with Mr. Time Bomb:

The very first thing you need to do is not blame yourself for his actions or lack of actions. There is absolutely nothing you can do to control another person's emotions and Mr. Time Bomb is typically an emotional wreck. His inability to respond or express his emotions is at the root of his outburst. With this being said please understand that in no way are we condoning a physically, verbally, or emotionally abusive relationship. *If you are being abused please get out and get help.* We also are not condoning a man having an affair nor are we stating that you are responsible for your man cheating on you. But the reality is if the home environment is perceived as a war zone most individuals will look for a safe refuge. This often times results in a relationship of some form with another person outside of the home.

Your responsibility is to know who you are in a relationship with and learn how to communicate with him in a way that will be received so that the relationship can flourish, I'm not saying that you cater to his every whim, but you don't pick fights just for the heck of it. Learn to speak his language so that he can hear your request and concerns. Many times when dealing with the passive-aggressive man we tend to think if we match testosterone with them it will make them move. Ladies I have a secret for you, I don't care how strong you are or how loud you are, or how much quicker with words you are -- you will never have more testosterone, in other words your balls are not bigger than his. He may just put them away when you are in the room but he will pull them out when backed in a corner or he will pull them out when he feels safe.

This simply means that if you know your man doesn't handle confrontation well then don't scream down on him as soon as he walks into the door from work. If you have an issue that needs to be talked about you need to create an environment that will make him feel safe and comfortable so that you can share your concerns without attacking each other. This may be challenging in the beginning and it may even take counseling to learn how to communicate effectively. Men typically do not have the capacity to receive as many words daily as women do. Women can talk and talk all day at work, come home and continue to vent about their day, what went wrong with the kids, and how the dishwasher doesn't work. Men deal with their bosses and co-workers at work all day and listen to them and their complaints. So when they get home they are looking for a safe refuge where they can get some down time before having to hear another list of what went wrong and what they did wrong. So it is important that you pick the time that you share your concerns so they can be heard and received.

Mr. Time Bomb can sometimes be a silent exploder, which means he may act out his frustrations by engaging in illicit and self-destructive behavior, such as, alcohol abuse, drug use, pornography or even engaging in an extramarital affair. These are the extremes and he may not engage in such obvious behavior but if you suspect that he has an alcohol or drug problem or is he engaged in pornography or is having an affair it is best to address these issues immediately. Denial does no one any good and the sooner the truth is out the better for all involved. I strongly recommend you seek the counsel of a professional counselor or therapist to help you deal with these issues to come up with a plan that will best help you and your family begin the healing process.

If he is physically or verbally abusive do not stay in a situation where your life or the lives of your children are in danger. Once in a safe place seek counseling and then try to work on a solution that best fits your family. I've seen cases where once the woman leaves the man is willing to seek counseling to get his anger under control and they are able to restore the relationship. It is less likely that if he has hit you once that he will never hit you again without getting any help. So please get help immediately if you are in an abusive relationship by calling the Domestic Violence Hotline: 800-621-HOPE (4673).

Tips for dealing with Mr. Time Bomb:

Well put sweetheart, you are absolutely correct in describing Mr. Time Bomb. If you think of a time bomb it detonates when the time is up. Which means as long as you are hearing the ticking then the bomb is still alive. In order to get the ticking to stop it must be defused. The reason why I say this is because for most of my life, I was that guy. The ticking represented the stuff on my chest, in my head - the pressure that I felt but had no way to express. When I say no way to express it, I didn't know how to say it, so most often I wouldn't talk about anything deep. I wouldn't talk about my feelings, I wouldn't talk about what I really thought, and if I did talk about it, I certainly wasn't going to share it with the person or people who it affected the most. When a time bomb is allowed to continue to tick this way eventually there is an explosion. For me that explosion looked like the destruction of my first marriage. After twelve years it ended in divorce and although adultery on my part was a factor,

I now understand that my lack of dealing with issues in my previous marriage was the fuel that led me down a path of infidelity that ultimately destroyed my marriage.

If there is one tip I can give you when dealing with Mr. Time Bomb it is to please pay attention to what you see. You are not crazy! When a talkative man can't talk to you, there is a problem. When he puts everything under the sun before you, there is a problem. When he chooses to create ways to spend time outside of the house, there is a problem. Stop dealing with the symptoms and start trying to get to the root of the problem. Mr. Time Bomb really wants to be defused however it's going to take time and work to do it properly. Rather than spend your energy and focus on what he's not doing, pay attention and praise what he is doing. My wife said it best, if you can create an environment that encourages him to share he will give you insight on how he ticks, you just have to be willing to put that kind of energy into the relationship.

In my first marriage no one ever taught my ex-wife how to create an environment that encouraged me to share. I am not blaming the failure of our marriage on her,

I played a major part in the destruction of our relationship and I've since apologized to her a million times and we are really cool today. This only came as a result of me coming to the conclusion that I didn't know how to handle my emotions properly. Even though it wasn't in time to save my first marriage it came at the perfect time for me to be able to help raise our son in the most beautiful blended family unit I've ever seen.

7

MR. SENSITIVE

All the ladies love Mr. Sensitive. He is a great listener and he has a heart of gold. He may have grown up in a house full of women or was raised by a strong mother so he can understand your pain. In some cases he may be very close with his mother, but he could be resentful towards her. He can either be a lover of women or a women lover. The lover of women has learned how a woman ticks from his exposure to caring for a woman with his mother. He may have been the little boy who his mother treated like her little man. She catered to his every whim and she doted on him constantly. She also confided in him about her life so he became her best friend. Thus he learned how women think and what their buttons are emotionally.

The other side of Mr. Sensitive is the women lover. He may have been raised to care for his mother. This can be the result of his mother working long hours, suffering from illness or drug abuse, which often results in his winding up being the caretaker in the home. This taught him how to take care for a woman's basic needs but not her emotional needs. He may have grown up as a womanizer and may have found it difficult to settle down in a committed relationship.

In both of these cases he has learned how to care for others with a feminine slant. Men are supposed to be logical thinkers and not emotionally driven, but Mr. Sensitive can allow his emotions to lead him. His emotional attachment to people and things clouds his logical thinking which makes it hard for him to lead his family. Now don't get me wrong not many women want a man who is unemotional and is uncaring, but there are times when one of you has to be able to put their emotions aside and see things as they are.

How to live with Mr. Sensitive:

Over time the very things that attracted you to him can become deterrents. In the beginning you may have admired how passionate he would be about a topic when he discussed it but this has now become a source for many of your arguments. He is so passionate about his opinion or his wants that he is unable to see the forest for the trees, which causes him to get stuck on an idea and unable to see from anyone else's viewpoint. If he is a typical Mr. Sensitive, he wears his emotions on his sleeves and it can become difficult for you to share how you really feel because you are concerned about how it will make him feel. This is where you have to put on your big girl pants and speak truth in love. You are not responsible for how he feels but you are responsible for being honest with him. If you dislike something that he is doing the worst thing that you can do is not say something because you are concerned with how it will make him feel.

Life is not fair and if he doesn't hear the truth from the person who loves him imagine how much harder it will be for him to hear it from a total stranger. You actually do him a disservice by not being honest. Sure his feelings may be hurt but in time he will realize that you are only telling him the truth because you love him. Unfortunately he did not hear a whole lot of truth when he was growing up. He was accustomed to hearing how cute he was or how bright he was or how special he was. His mother learned early that he was sensitive so rather than upset him she sugar-coated things or just ignored them. He may get angry when things don't go his way because he is used to always having his way. The worst thing you can do is continue this. When you disagree you have to tell him. If you don't want to go to the movies tell him. Don't just go along because you think he will get upset. You have to remember that Mr. Sensitive allows his emotions to run him at times so he is prone to fits of emotional outburst. He may be a fusser or a pouter, either way his emotions cause him to respond emotionally to situations rather than make rational decisions when he is emotionally charged. It is hard for him to let things go when he feels that he is wronged but he can easily let things go when he wrongs someone else because in his mind he has won. This can be very frustrating in a relationship, but it is not impossible to deal with.

You have to remember that you are not responsible for how someone feels, you are responsible for clearly communicating your thoughts about an issue and you have the right to have a different opinion than your mate. This is the hardest part of dealing with Mr. Sensitive. As women we are nurturers the last thing we want to do is hurt those we love. That is why you must constantly remind yourself that you are only sharing how you feel or think. As long as you do it in love then you are not responsible for their reaction or how they feel about what you have said. It may take time for you to see a change in how he responds. Eventually he will realize that you love him, you're not trying to hurt him, and that it's okay to have different opinions. Most men don't really want a woman who just goes along with everything they say or want to do. They want a woman who has her own mind and has her own opinions. This may be hard for Mr. Sensitive to accept this difference initially. Stay true to you and in time he will appreciate your differences, accept them, and even look forward to healthy debates on your differing opinions.

Tips for dealing with Mr. Sensitive:

It is very difficult for me to add to what my wife has already said. She has really summed up who Mr. Sensitive is. In her ability to detach from certain emotions she was able to create an environment that did not give in to my being overly sensitive. This is very important. Whether you know it or not, you have the ability to take the emotion out of a room. The best way to do this is to not add fuel to the fire. Just as fire needs oxygen Mr. Sensitive needs your emotional connection to keep him going. My wife was able to demonstrate what it looked like when people said *"get over it"*, without having to say get over it. And the way she did that was by intentionally not taking part in my emotional tirades.

I remember one time when we went to Florida on vacation when I was in rare form. We got to the resort and after checking into our room my wife to started complaining that the room was not warm enough for her. In my mind, I'm thinking this is Florida, how warm do you need it to be. Yes, Mr. Sensitive can be a jerk as well.

Emotionally I began to feel pushed to do something I didn't want to do, which was simple to change rooms even though we had already unpacked. We eventually changed rooms but I was unhappy because it caused me to be inconvenienced. Later that evening my wife suggested we go on a drive to a restaurant to clear the funk in the air. But of course I didn't want to drop the matter and I continued to fuss and argue anyway. I noticed that my wife chose not to argue back with me, which was the first time I had ever witnessed somebody discharging the atmosphere of emotion by simply not responding. I wish I could say that it worked that time, but it didn't. As the night went on I continued to stew in my anger, but now it was because she would not argue with me. I said some very hurtful things to her and she stood her ground and refused to argue with me.

That day was when I learned that it takes two to tango and without words her actions began to influence me to change my behavior if I wanted to have a healthy relationship with her. It took me several days to get past my emotions at the time, but because of my wife's stance I respect her space today, and although we have disagreements we do not violently argue - Period. We don't go back and forth, that was the last screaming match that I had with myself.

The bottom line is when dealing with Mr. Sensitive you cannot match emotion with him you have to do the opposite. Meaning that if he is down in the dumps then you can't go down there with him or if he is pouting and ranting about an issue you cannot feed the fire by adding energy to the issue. Mr. Sensitive has a tendency to take everything personal and you cannot feed into this. Stick to the facts and over time he will get tired of fussing alone and will learn to use his inside voice and not see every disagreement as a personal attack.

Living With A Momma's Boy

8

BREAKING THE CYCLE

If you are a mother and you recognize any of these qualities in your son do not despair. This is not a time to feel guilty or blame but it is time to put some things in place to help position your son so that he can grow into a man. Whether you have been forced to raise him on your own because of the absence of his father or you are the dominant parent in the household there are some things you can do to help him get the manhood training he needs.

The first thing to do is STOP controlling his every move. I know as a parent that it is often easier to raise children in a controlled environment, one that you can control the outcome of as much as possible. NEWS FLASH - you absolutely cannot control another person, you may be able to get them to do what you want them to do out of fear but if your goal is to teach them how to be a healthy functional adult this will only get them so far. The key to success is failure. If you do not allow your son to fail he will never learn how to succeed at anything.

Begin to give him responsibility around your home, and make it age appropriate to teach him to become self-reliant. It is not age appropriate for a five year old to have to cook dinner, but is perfectly appropriate for him to make his bed and put up his clothes. Now I know you are saying he can't make the bed up the way I want it to be done, but this is not about what you want it is about teaching him to be responsible. No woman wants to marry a man who cannot take care of himself and unfortunately many of us have been blessed with these men and wonder why their mothers didn't teach them the simple things in life. Don't be one of those mothers. You are raising a man, so keep this in mind at every stage of your sons' development. He must be able to pull his own weight and this means playing an active part in the family and not merely being a spectator who is served.

Teach him how to be selfless by having him do service work, such as feeding the homeless on the weekend or cutting the lawn of an elderly neighbor for free. Rather than giving him everything that he wants, such as the latest Jordan's teach him to earn the things he wants. This can be done by rewarding him for good grades or by giving him an allowance for household chores rather than being his automatic ATM whenever he wants something. Teaching him the value of money and the value of hard work are qualities that he needs as a man.

If his father is not present or actively involved get your son involved in organized sports or a youth organization that focuses on character building and brotherhood. Boys need the example of men to learn how to be men, just as you can't demonstrate for him how to pee standing up there are certain characteristics of a man he can only learn from being in the presence of a man.

Choose men who have the character that you desire for your son to have. If these men are not your man, I admonish you to keep your own boundaries and allow this man to build a relationship with your son without your building a relationship with him. In my years of working with youth, one of the worst things I have seen a mother do is to get into a relationship with the man who is mentoring her son. Once a boy builds a trust in a man and is able to confide in him the things he can't confide in his mother it is a violation of that trust for the man to now engage in a relationship with his mother. If he is not already your man then go find another man. Now I am not saying that you let your son be in relationship with a complete stranger, but I am saying don't cloud the situation by becoming romantically involved with his coach, teacher, or mentor.

Lastly I encourage you to use "reality discipline" with your son. In Kevin Leman's book "Running The Rapids" he talks about teaching your children that there are consequences and rewards for their actions. If your son comes to you at 8 o'clock pm and tells you that he needs supplies to do a project for school that is due in the morning, the proper response is to allow him to suffer the consequence of not preparing in advance even if this results in a failing grade. It is not your responsibility to run out to the store at 8 o'clock, get the supplies and sit up with him all night to complete his project. We all know this really means you doing the project because he needs to go to sleep and get rest for the next day at school. I was guilty of this myself when my son came to live with us in the eighth grade. I quickly learned that I was causing more harm than good by not allowing him to reap the consequences of his actions.

When we step in and fix their messes we teach them that they do not have to be responsible and that mommy will always fix it. Reality discipline is telling your son that the consequence of his hitting his sister will be his having to do her chores for a week and sticking to it. It is not being extreme and issuing consequences that you are not going to uphold. Be careful not to issue sentences that you are not prepared to keep, such as grounding him for three months for failing a test. For one the punishment does not match the offense and in most cases you will forget why you issued this sentence in the first place three weeks down the road because inevitably he will have committed other offenses that overshadows the initial offense. And the truth is he knows you can't keep that going when you say it and it causes him to lose respect for your threats.

I know many of us grew up in an age where our parents spanked us and grounding was the rule. I am not saying that there are not times when a pat on the bottom is not appropriate but when your son hits his sister, you hit him, and tell him that hitting is unacceptable. What are you really teaching him? Just a thought.

Reality discipline is about teaching your son that every decision he makes will result in either a reward or consequence. When he completes his chores he will get a reward in the form of an allowance or a privilege. With our son we would grant the privilege of playing a video game or watching TV for thirty minutes on a school night for the completion of nightly chores or for earning an A or B on a test or quiz.

If your son isn't still of school age it is not too late. The older he is it may take more effort but you can begin to turn the tide and help him develop the necessary skills to become a responsible and caring man. As I stated before do not beat yourself up if you instilled some Momma's Boy traits in your son, simply begin today to teach him some new things and watch the character of a man begin to develop in your son.

9

FINAL THOUGHTS

Now that we have shared with you our perspective and tips on how to live with a Momma's Boy, I hope that you were able to be encouraged and have some tools to help you move forward. I have shared with you some of the challenges I experienced living with the Momma's Boys in my life. I admit that it has been challenging at times and there were times when I wanted to run, but I love both of my recovering Momma's Boys and wouldn't trade them for anything in the world.

Let me be clear, men and women are different and no matter whether he was raised in a "good home" or he is a product of the foster care system, you will have challenges in your relationship. Whenever you bring two people together who were raised in different homes, they will have some different expectations, beliefs, and values. I am an optimist and I believe that most relationships can succeed if both parties are willing to put in the work and are willing to compromise. The thing to remember is that any relationship takes work, so if you are in a relationship with a Momma's Boy don't give up on him, think of him as a diamond in the rough. In most cases you probably saw his potential when you met, and know that you can identify some of his behavior you are better equipped on how to deal with him.

Now there may be some of you, in a relationship with a Momma's Boy whose issues may require you to make a decision regarding the status of the relationship. If the relationship has escalated to the level of physical abuse, you have to determine if the situation is safe for you and your children. As we previously stated we do not condone any form of abuse and recommend that you seek professional help immediately in order to deal with any form of abuse, whether verbal, emotional, or physical.

For those single ladies who are dating I want to give you a few things to look for in order to help you better identify the Momma's Boy so that you can be prepared for some of the challenges you may encounter with him if you choose to pursue a relationship. I know you have all heard that how a man treats his mother will be an indication of how he will treat you. I want to also encourage you to look at his relationship or lack of a relationship with his father. If his father was absent there is a chance that he may not have received all the manhood training men with fathers get. You will also want to look at what types of things he was interested in as a child and teen. If he was involved in any type of organized sport, boy scouts, or things along this nature then there is a good chance that he received some coaching from a man during those crucial years of adolescents which may have helped to properly shape his manhood. However the following is a list of a few tell-tale signs that he may have missed out on that kind of training.

❖ He gets significance out of being the center of attention *(self-centered)*

❖ He may not stand up for himself or you (*avoids conflicts*)

❖ He is indecisive (*doesn't want to rock the boat*)

❖ He overreacts to small things (*wears his emotions on his sleeves*)

These are just a few things for you to pay attention to when you are dating. Men who are raised with a healthy male influence learn how to be selfless, confront issues, walk confidently, and handle their emotions properly. When they miss training in any of these areas they can have some Momma's Boy tendencies. Please note that these signs are not a guarantee that he is a Momma's Boy, but it will help you to recognize certain areas of his character.

If you are in a relationship with a grown Momma's Boy who displays the qualities of a boy you have to remember he may be a man in age – but may emotionally be a boy trapped in a man's body. This could be your boss, co-worker, or friend but if you approach it from that perspective you will realize that he has issues and not take his deficiencies personal. Remember you didn't create him and therefore you can't change him. It is not your personal responsibility to fix him, but you can learn to respect him and work with him with a better understanding of who he is.

If you are married, dating, or engaged to your Momma's Boy and you have done all you can do to try to relate to him and he still is not willing to put you and your family in their proper place then you have to commit to focus on you and the well being of your children. We would recommend that you seek professional counseling to help you sort through the challenges in your relationship. As a word of advice be honest with yourself and be honest about your situation. Denial will not help to correct any areas that need adjusting. Our hope is that you are able to take the tips we have shared and are able to learn to love and live with your Momma's Boy long enough to see him recover. The key is recovering. Just like an addict as long as they remain in their addiction we can either be an enabler or we can put boundaries in place which will either help them to seek recovery or distance themselves from unhealthy people in their lives.

If the Momma's Boy in your life is your son then you are in a great position because you can now help to change the course of his life by setting boundaries and expectations to help him develop into a man, along with connecting him with positive male role models to help foster his maleness. Even if he is grown if you have a solid relationship you can still help to influence him so that his future family will have a fighting chance.

If your Momma's Boy is a friend or casual acquaintance you are in the greatest position, in that you are not obligated or committed to them and if they are not willing to accept the boundaries you set in place you can walk away from the relationship and get on with your life if you choose to.

Living With A Momma's Boy

RESOURCES

Joyce Meyer, *Approval Addiction: Overcoming Your Need to Please Everyone* (FaithWords; Reprint edition (November 3, 2008)

P. D. Eastman, *Are You My Mother?* (Random House Books for Young Readers; 1 edition
(June 12, 1960)

Henry Cloud and John Townsend, *Boundaries: When to Say YES, When to Say NO, To Take Control of Your Life* (Zondervan; Revised edition (October 20, 1992)

Coming to America (Eddie Murphy Productions, Paramount Pictures (1988)

Glenn P. Brooks Jr., *How To Raise A Man.. Not A ·Momma's Boy!* (CreateSpace Independent Publishing Platform (November 3, 2011)

Scott Wetzler, *Living with the Passive-Aggressive Man: Coping with Hidden Aggression – From the Bedroom to the Boardroom* (Touchstone (October 1, 1993)

John Gray, PHD., *Men Are from Mars, Women Are from Venus: The Classic Guide to Understanding the*

Opposite Sex (Harper Paperbacks; Reprint edition (January 6, 2004)

Harriet B. Braiker, *The Disease to Please: Curing the People Pleaser Syndrome*
(McGraw-Hill; 1 edition (February 13, 2002)

Michael Maccoby, *The Productive Narcissist*
(Broadway (April 8, 2003)

H. Norman Wright, *Understanding the Man in Your Life* (Thomas Nelson (August 29, 1989)

About the Authors:

Sheri A. Brooks and Glenn P. Brooks, Jr.

Sheri is a relationship coach, author, social services professional and a student of human behavior and psychology. She is an advocate for healthy and functional families. Through her life experiences she has been able to help other women to avoid the pitfalls of failed marriages and self-destructive behavior to reach their full potential as women who are more than a mother or a wife, but an individual.

Glenn is an author, motivational speaker, relationship and parenting coach, and voice over talent. With over 20 years of experience working in the lives of youth, parents and couples helping to equip them with the tools to have healthy and functional relationships.

They are the founders of Glenn P Brooks Jr LLC and Constant Relationship Coaching which focuses on inspiring, teaching, and coaching.

Living With A Momma's Boy

For more information

Visit us on the web to learn about coaching and consultant services
www.GlennPBrooksJr.com
www.ConstantRelationshipCoaching.com

Check out other titles by the authors

How To Raise A Man …
Not A Momma's Boy
By Glenn P. Brooks, Jr

Managing Students Through
Relationships NOT Rules
By Glenn P. Brooks, Jr.

The Journey From Rejection To
Significance
By Sheri A. Brooks

Made in the USA
Las Vegas, NV
07 November 2022

58972049R00088